GIRLS'GUIDES

InfoGirl

A Girl's Guide to the Internet

Marty Brown

the rosen publishing group's
rosen central
new york

For Ruthie and Bethie, my favorite sisters, and for Rachel, who rules.

Special thanks to Erin, Alex, and Mike for their patience and support.

Published in 1999 by The Rosen Publishing Group, Inc.
29 East 21st Street, New York, New York 10010

First Edition

Library of Congress Cataloging-in-Publication Data

Brown, Marty, 1966-
    Infogirl : a girl's guide to the Internet / Marty Brown.
        p. cm. — (Girls' guides)
    Includes bibliographical references and index.
    Summary: Describes the Internet's history, features, and uses and suggests ways for girls to get involved on-line.
    ISBN 0-8239-2984-1 (lib. bdg.)
    1. Girls' computer network resources—United States Juvenile literature. [1. Internet (Computer network)] I. Title. II. Series.
ZA4201.B76 1999
025.04—dc21
99-25120
CIP

Manufactured in the United States of America

Contents

About This Book

The middle school years are like a roller coaster—wild and scary but also fun and way cool. One minute you're way, way up there, and the next minute you're plunging down into the depths. Not surprisingly, sometimes you may find yourself feeling confused and lost. Not to worry, though. Just like on a roller-coaster ride, at the end of all this crazy middle school stuff, you'll be laughing and screaming and talking about how awesome it all was.

Right now, however, chances are your body is changing so much that it's barely recognizable, your old friends may not share your interests anymore, and your life at school is suddenly hugely complicated. And let's not even get into the whole boy issue. It's a wonder that you can still think straight at all.

Fortunately, reader dear, help is here. This book is your road map. It's also a treasure chest filled with ideas and advice. Armed with this book and with your own inner strength (trust us, you have plenty), you can safely, confidently navigate the twists and turns of your middle school years. It will be tough going, and sometimes you'll wonder if you'll ever get through it. But you—fabulous, powerful, unique you—are up to the task. This book is just a place to start.

The Inter-What?

You're hanging out in your favorite chat room, talking to your buds about the concert last Friday night, when you hear a familiar sound. The e-mail symbol flashes across your computer screen. "BRB"— "Be right back"—you type and go to your e-mail. It's a message from your Italian pen pal telling you to check out a really hot Web site. You glance at the clock in the corner of your screen. Your parents let you spend only one hour a day on the Internet, and you still have some research to do for a history paper. So much to do, so little time . . .

Like many girls, you may have discovered all the cool stuff on the Internet. Or maybe you surf the Net once in a while but want to know more about what you can do there. Or

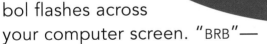

Cyberspace: Another word for the Internet.

maybe you think the Internet sounds really neat, but you're not sure where to start.

Unless you've been living under a rock for the past few years, you've probably heard a lot about the Net, even if you aren't yet on-line. You may have heard that it's a great place to get information, find good stuff, and meet new people. It is. On the Internet you can do all these things and more.

Way Back When

What exactly is the Internet? It's not as complicated as it sounds. Basically it's just a bunch of computers connected together.

The United States Department of Defense started the Internet in 1969. They were afraid a war with the Soviet Union would begin and wanted a means of communication that still would work even after a nuclear attack. That's why they created the Internet. Back then the Internet was called the ARPANET, short for Advanced Research Project Agency Network.

Digerati: A collective term for forward-looking, high-minded users of technology.

A nuclear attack never happened. However, ARPANET caught on and stuck around because it was such an easy way for people with computers to communicate. The United States Department of Defense added more computers, and the network grew. In 1984 the National

Netizen: A citizen of the Internet.

Science Foundation jumped on board and joined ARPANET with five supercomputer centers. Supercomputers (like the one on the right) are very large, fast computers that scientists often use. ARPANET gave access to any university or government agency that wanted it.

In the mid-eighties, ARPANET became very big. Instead of connecting, or networking, individual computers together, computer scientists started networking the networks together. They called it the Inter-Network-Network, which soon got shortened to the Internet, or just the Net.

Today the Internet is an enormous network of networks that connects the whole world. Every day millions of people use the Internet for communication, research, business, shopping, and entertainment. Some people are so used to surfing the Net that it seems second nature. At the same time, the Internet is still very new. It can be confusing, scary, and hard to navigate. It's a little bit like the Wild West. There's a lot of territory to explore, but there isn't always a clear road to travel.

Newbie: A newcomer to the Internet. Everyone starts out as a newbie.

Lay of the Land

2

So how's lil' ol' you going to make your way through cyberspace? After all, there's a whole wide world out there, and you haven't got a road map.

To navigate more easily, you can break the Internet down into three big territories. As you start your Internet adventure, you'll want to become familiar with them all.

The Web

When people talk about the Internet today, more often than not, they're talking about the World Wide Web. The Web was developed in the late eighties by scientists at CERN (the European Lab for Particle Physics) as an easy way to find and display documents on the Internet. Before the Web, it was a lot harder to find your way around on the Internet.

What makes the Web very useful and really cool is that documents, or pages, are tied together with connections called hypertext links. When you click on a link, it takes you to another document. A Web page can have an unlimited number of links to documents all over the world. A Web site is a group of related Web pages linked together.

Another great feature of the Web is that it's not limited to just text. Web pages can include images, sound, video, and even small computer applications called applets. An applet is a miniature program on a Web page. Games and calculators are two of the most common types of applets on the Web, doing almost anything from playing chess to calculating how much you would weigh on the moon.

The science brains at CERN probably had no idea how popular the Web would become. It's the number one destination for fun and entertainment on the Internet. You're sure to be spending a lot of time there.

Meetin' and Greetin' People

All sorts of ways exist to communicate over the Internet. E-mail and chat are two of the coolest. E-mail lets you use your computer to write messages that are delivered instantly to anywhere in the world. Chat (also known as IRC, or Internet relay chat) allows you to have written "conversations" in special areas of the Internet called chat rooms.

E-mail and chat are the most popular ways to communicate on the Net. But other ways are just as good, such as Usenet and listservs. We'll soon explore all of them in chapter four.

Finding What You Want

Sure, it's fun to surf the Web and hang out with cyber-friends. But the Internet has lots of practical uses too. For instance, it's a great place to turn for help with homework. By using search engines and gopher servers—which you'll read about later—you'll be able to access the same information that professors and research scientists use. No matter how you

Everything You've Ever Needed to Know. . . And More!

MTV http://www.mtv.com
On-line version of the popular TV channel.

Music Fan Clubs Organization http://www.musicfanclubs.org
Information on all your favorite artists and groups.

Paramount Pictures http://paramount.com
Tons of stuff on Paramount's movies and TV shows.

The World Around You

City Search
http://www.citysearch.com
Everything you ever wanted to know about almost every city in the United States.

Map Quest
http://www.mapquest.com
Pick any place in the world, and a map will pop up on your screen. You can even create a street map that shows where you live.

The Weather Channel
http://www.weather.com
Check out the weather around the world.

search, everything you need to know is at your fingertips.

It won't take long to become a pro at finding what you're looking for. Then you can take that set of outdated encyclopedias and use it for something useful. Like a doorstop.

Okay. Now you know what the Internet is and what it can do for you. So how do you join the digerati? Well, first you have to get connected.

Powerful People

Canada's Parliament http://www.parl.gc.ca/index.html
Read in either French or English.

U.S. Senators http://iecc.com/senate.html
E-mail addresses for all U.S. senators listed alphabetically by state.

U.S. Congresspersons http://iecc.com/house.html
E-mail addresses for all U.S. congresspersons listed alphabetically by state.

The White House http://whitehouse.gov
All sorts of information about the nation's most famous residence.

Get Wired!

3

Before you start having fun, hanging out, and getting the info you want on the Internet, you have to get some high-tech gear, and you have to get connected.

Computer Basics

When you think of a computer, what you probably picture is the computer hardware. Hardware is all the physical bits and pieces that make up your computer. But before we say too much about hardware, you should know a few basic computer terms.

Central Processing Unit (CPU) This is found inside your computer. Think of it as your computer's brain. CPUs operate at different speeds. The higher the number, the faster the processor—and the faster the better.

Hard drive The place where files are stored on your computer. Think of this as storage space, like a closet.

Random Access Memory (RAM) RAM is what your computer uses to retrieve and process information. If your hard drive is a filing cabinet, RAM is your staff of file clerks. RAM is measured in megabytes. The more RAM you have, the better and faster your computer works.

Monitor The computer screen.

Hardware, or the Expensive Stuff

An Internet connection won't do you any good if you don't have a computer. Duh! You don't need the newest, fastest, coolest computer to get on-line. However, there are a few pieces of hardware that you just have to have. The first is the computer itself.

You can connect to the Internet using either an IBM-compatible personal computer (PC) or a Macintosh computer. Every computer runs on a certain operating system, which basically tells the computer what to do and how and when to do it. If you're using a PC, you'll have a lot more fun if you're running the Microsoft Windows operating system. Windows 95 or 98 is the best. If you're using a Macintosh, you'll want System 7.5 or higher.

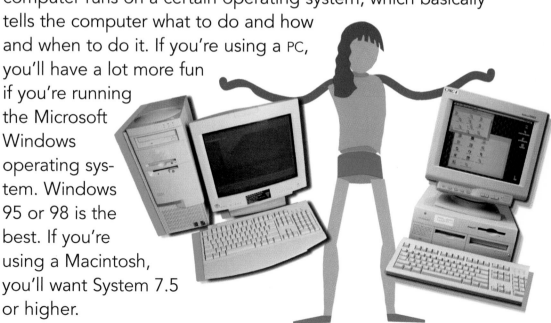

When you're getting connected, you'll need at least 16 megabytes of RAM. If you have 32 megabytes it's even better—64, and you're set for life. Or at least for the next two weeks. There's no such thing as too much RAM.

You'll also want the fastest modem you can get. A modern modem's speed is measured in kilobits per second (Kbps, or just "K"). Basically, the higher the number, the faster the modem. You can limp along with a 14.4-Kbps modem. A 28.8K modem is good, and 56K is the best. Old modems used measurements called bauds or bps (bits per second) and some connected to phone lines using the receiver of a regular telephone. If you have a 9600 bps modem, donate it to a museum!

This 9600 bps modem is practically a fossil now.

Software—The Cheaper Stuff

Once you've got hardware, you'll also need some basic software on your computer. Software is the term for any application or program. Software sends instructions to your hardware, enabling your computer to actually do stuff.

The software that your modem needs to talk to the Internet is called dialup software. It is already part of your computer's operating system. In Windows, it's called dialup networking. On a Macintosh, it has two parts: Mac TCP/IP and PPP.

On some newer systems, all of this is called remote access. Look at the help files on your computer to get these set up.

After your dialup software, probably the single most important thing to have is a Web browser, like Netscape Navigator or Microsoft Internet Explorer. A Web browser is a computer program, also known as an application, that helps you navigate the Web. Once you have a Web browser, you can download just about any other software you need. "Download" means to copy a file off the Internet onto your computer. Most Internet service providers (ISPs) give you browser software when you sign up.

Web browsers have some cool perks, too. For example, Netscape Navigator and Internet Explorer both have built-in e-mail programs. Many computers come with a Web browser and an e-mail program already installed, or put into the computer, so check to see if you have one.

You also can buy software packages that promise everything you need to connect to the Internet. But be warned:

Don't be too quick to hand over your cash. Before you buy one of these packages, remember that most of the software you need is available for free on the Internet. Also, most ISPs will give you free software when you sign up for their service. They'll also help you learn how to use it.

Getting Connected

You already know the basics: The Internet is really nothing more than a bunch of computers networked together and connected by wires and cables, much like telephone and cable television systems.

Some computers are permanently connected to the Internet by cables. Others use phone lines to make temporary connections. If you access the Internet through a library or classroom, the computer you're using probably has a dedicated, or permanent, connection to the Internet. If you want to connect to the Internet from your home, you'll use a modem. Unless your house is wired for the next century, you'll need the modem to "dial up" and connect to the Internet over your phone line. Since your computer is using the phone line, you can't make phone calls while you're on-line. You can dial up and chat with your buds on-line or call them on the phone,

Handshake: The funny sound your modem makes when it's connecting to the Internet.

but you can't do both at the same time.

So what does "dial up" mean? Sounds technical, huh? It's pretty simple. When you use a modem to dial up the Internet, all you're doing is connecting your computer by phone line to a computer that in turn is connected to the Net.

Confused yet? Don't worry. All you need to remember is that some computers are permanently connected to the Internet, and others aren't. Odds are yours isn't. So you'll need an Internet service provider.

Internet Service Providers

Internet service providers provide dialup access to the Internet. Their costs and services vary, but most will give you unlimited time on the Internet for about twenty bucks a month. You can choose from tons of ISPs—everything from national ISPs to small, locally owned services run out of basements and garages.

Some ISPs are better than others. Their quality has almost nothing to do with their size but has everything to do with their equipment, connection speed, technical skill, and

To Get Hooked Up, Try....

America Online http://www.aol.com The most popular on-line service. It has chat rooms, e-mail, Web access, and a special area just for kids.

CompuServe http://www.compuserve.com Many of the same features as America Online.

The List http://thelist.internet.com Huge list of Internet service providers in the United States and Canada.

customer service. A small ISP
run from your neighbor's
garage can be better than a

huge, nationally known one. Don't be afraid to ask questions and shop around. One of the best ways to find a good ISP is to ask people who live near you what they use.

On-line services like America Online (AOL) and CompuServe are another option. The Internet is a public street where anyone can go, but on-line services are more like private clubs. You can't get in unless you're a member. On-line services offer features such as chat rooms and electronic magazines that are available only to members. On-line services are very easy to use, which makes them a good option for Internet newbies.

It used to be that on-line services weren't even connected to the Net. Today all major on-line services offer full Internet access. However, their access is sometimes slower than what you get from an ISP, especially at peak times. When a lot of members try to get out of the private club and onto the public street through the same doors at the same time, bottlenecks and traffic jams happen.

Okay, you've got the hardware, you've got the software, and you're connected. Let's go, girl! Now that you're ready to start surfing through cyberspace, you'll want to get hooked up with some of your buds and find some cool sites. After all, it's not as though you got this computer just to help with your homework, right? You want to have some fun!

4

E-mail@YourAddress.net

E-mail, short for electronic mail, is one of the oldest uses of the Internet, an it's still one of the most popular. It's faster than sending a letter, and it's a lot less expensive than a long-

distance phone call. If you have friends who have moved away or if you're interested in making friends outside of your hometown, you'll want to memorize your e-mail address right away. You'll be using it a lot.

There are many e-mail software programs out there, like Communicator and Outlook Express, and they're all a little bit different. E-mail is so easy to send and receive that you'll get the hang of it in no time flat, no matter what software you use. Just type your crush's e-mail address in the "to" or "recipient" field, type a few words in the subject field so he knows what the e-mail is about, then let your fingers fly in the message field. When you're done, click "send." It's that simple.

All e-mail addresses include a symbol that means "at." It looks like this: @. Every address has two parts. The part before the @ is your mailbox name. The second part is the name of the domain, or area of the Internet, where the mailbox is located. Let's say that you have an account at Girl Power Internet Service. Their domain name is girlpower.net, and your account name is janedoe. Your e-mail address would be *janedoe@girlpower.net.* You say it as, "jane-doe at girlpower dot net."

You probably noticed that domain names have different endings, like .com, .edu, and .net. These domain names are called top-level domains, or zones. Some zones are organizational, meaning they describe what a place does. These include .com for commercial and .gov for government. Others are geographical domains, like .us for the United States and .ca for Canada. As you hang out on the Internet, you'll get to know what different domains are all about.

No, Not Girls—URLS

The Web uses domain names too. To go somewhere on the Web, type a URL (uniform resource locator) into your Web browser. A URL is really just the address of the site or file you are requesting. It always starts with the prefix "http://" followed by the domain name and the name of the file. Most Web domains start with "www."

For example: "http://www.health.org/gpower/index.htm" tells your Web browser to "use the hypertext transport protocol (http) to go to the World Wide Web domain (www) called health.org. Look for the file called index.htm in the directory called gpower."

Whaaat?

Are you completely confused? If so, you're not alone. URLs can be really long and crazy sometimes. That's why Web browsers have an awesome feature called bookmarks (or favorites). Bookmarks work sort of like the speed dial on your telephone. Instead of typing in the whole long URL, just select the page from a list of page names, and your Web browser will know where to go.

Listservs and Usenet

If you want to make some cyberfriends but aren't sure how to start, try using a listserv. A listserv is an e-mail discussion that's sent only to

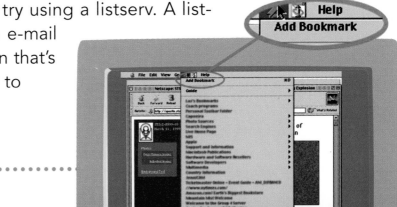

members. You join by signing up for one. Don't worry; it's free. Listservs usually talk about a specific subject or interest, like pets, fashion, or just about anything else.

A listserv will come to your e-mail address like any other e-mail, but it's really a written conversation between lots of different people. When you subscribe to a listserv, you get the ability to post, or add, to the list as well as read it. Everyone who subscribes to the list can read your message.

A ListMaster or ListAdmin is usually in charge of a listserv. The ListMaster keeps track of all of the subscribers and their addresses. Depending on the list, the ListMaster also may write messages or monitor the postings to keep people talking about the list's subject.

Liszt Directory of E-mail Mailing Lists

http://www.liszt.com Search by category or keyword. Over 60,000 mailing lists on everything from dog grooming to Barbie dolls.

Usenet Info Center Launch Pad

http://sunsite.unc.edu/usenet-i/home.html Huge list of newsgroups as well as help with usenet commands.

There are thousands of lists on thousands of subjects, and they're a great way to get to know people who share your interests. You can "lurk" on a list (read without posting) until you feel comfortable introducing yourself. When you get a good idea of what the list is all about, join in.

Usenet groups are almost the same as listservs. The big difference is that the messages don't come to your e-mail address. Instead you go to a special place on the Internet to see them. Also, anyone can post to a Usenet group; you don't have to subscribe. There are even more Usenet groups than there are listservs. If you want to join a Usenet group, your ISP can help you.

Chat: Join the Party!

When you chat you have a computer conversation with someone in real time. This means that you "talk" back and forth together. But instead of talking, you type. Chatting is like going to a party. You show up, say hi to people you know, meet new people, and just hang out.

Unless you use AOL or a similar service, you usually need special software to chat.

Chat rooms can be confusing the first time you visit one. So many conversations are happening at once. It's like walking into a party where you don't know anyone. It's okay to lurk and eavesdrop on other people, but there's really no reason to be shy. Introduce yourself and join in a conversation that seems interesting. The next chapter, on netiquette, will give you some chatting tips on things like making friends, staying safe, and having fun.

Internet Relay Chat

Internet Tele-Cafe http://www.telecafe.com/telecafe Meet people from around the world in one of the largest on-line chat systems out there.

Netiquette

Way back in time, Miss Manners (that's her there on the right) used to dish out her advice on etiquette—rules about how to behave in social situations. She'd tell people, especially young women, things like which fork to use, how to set a "proper" dinner table, and how to write out a party invitation. Today the Internet has taken etiquette to a whole new level. It's called netiquette.

"Netiquette" is short for "Internet etiquette." Because the Internet is so new, it doesn't have many formal laws. A loose set of guidelines, called netiquette, helps Netizens conduct themselves in a civilized manner. Following the rules of netiquette will ensure that you make friends, not enemies. Here's the deal.

Stop the Spam!

There's one thing you need to remember about spam: Spam is bad. And it's not the stuff in the can at your grocery store.

Spam is the Net equivalent of junk mail. A spammer is someone who sends a huge number of e-mails, bogging down the Internet and people's personal computers. Spammers often send e-mail to hundreds of people at once. Every time someone responds to the message, even if it's just to complain about being spammed, the message goes to everyone on the e-mail list.

If you get spammed, delete the message right away. Don't respond, because that makes the problem worse. And if you're in doubt about whether or not to send something, don't do it.

Flaming Mad

When someone on the Internet gets angry and starts writing nasty, mean-spirited e-mails, it's called flaming. Flamers are operating at about the same level as a two-year-old who is having a temper tantrum. Flaming is silly, immature, and way lame.

Most flamers are just normal people who are having a bad day. However, if you hang out in chat rooms or on list-servs, you'll meet a hard-core flamer once in a while. When this happens, tell the chat room monitor or ListMaster, and let him or her handle it.

Some ISPs also will allow you to refuse e-mail from any address or domain you choose. If you do this, flamers can't get to you. But whatever you do, don't stoop to their level. The best thing to do is ignore them, and—like that two-year-old having the temper tantrum—they'll wear themselves out.

NO YELLING

Typing in all capital letters is called yelling. It's very rude. Once in a while, it may be appropriate to yell. Maybe you're talking about your crush, and you want to yell, "HE IS SO CUTE!" Okay, so sometimes you just HAVE to yell. But be very careful what you're yelling about and who you're yelling to. There's usually no need to shout.

Making Friends

Fat Cat Cafe http://www.fatcatcafe.com/kid/hobby
Talk to other kids about your hobbies.

Kidsphere Subscribe to: kidsphere@vms.cis.pitt.edu
Listserv for kids all over the planet.

Pen Pal Planet http://www.epix.net/~ppplanet/page7.html
Find a pen pal to exchange snail mail (old-fashioned, written) letters with.

Making Faces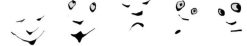

Did you know that you can draw pictures with your keyboard? Well, you can. They're called emoticons. Emoticons are little faces you can create using characters like letters and punctuation. You've probably seen this one before **: -)**

Emoticons

:) or :-)	Smile
:D	Big grin
**	Kisses
;) or ;-)	Wink
{}	Hug
:(or :-(	Frown
:'(	Crying
0:)	Angel
}:>	Devil
:X	Lips are sealed
:P	Tongue sticking out
:-!	Foot in mouth
:-]	Smirk
:\)	It's not funny
:-"	Lips pursed
|:-&	Angry
:-o	Shouting
:-@	Screaming
:-c	Really unhappy
:-x	Kissing

Acronyms Commonly Used in Chat and E-mail

ADN	Any day now
AFAIK	As far as I know
AFK	Away from keyboard
BAK	Back at keyboard
BRB	Be right back
CUL	See you later
DTRT	Do the right thing
FTF	Face to face
GAL	Get a life
GMTA	Great minds think alike
LTNS	Long time no see
LOL	Laughing out loud
ROTFL	Rolling on the floor laughing
TTFN	Ta-ta for now
WB	Welcome back
WTG	Way to go!

If you look at the picture sideways, you'll see two eyes, a nose, and a smiling mouth. There are hundreds of emoticons with as many expressions, and there's nothing to stop you from creating your own.

Emoticons show your facial expression or your tone of voice. When you're talking to people face-to-face, you can tell when they're being sarcastic or silly by the faces they make and the sound of their voice. Sometimes it's hard to tell those things on-line. To be sure that you're never misunderstood, use emoticons.

A Word of Warning

Maybe you'll meet someone on the Internet and become buds. Maybe you'll want to make plans to meet in person. If that happens, be smart and be safe.

One of the great things about the Internet is that nobody knows who you are. You're anonymous, or unknown. People have no way of knowing about the big zit on your nose or the bad haircut you got last week. You can try on different parts of your personality with people who don't already have ideas about who you are.

However, anonymity can be dangerous when it's abused. People can lie about who they are. Just because someone tells you that she's an eleven-year-old girl who likes horses and loves your favorite music group doesn't mean that it's true. That's why it's so important to use your smarts when you're on-line. You should never, ever, for any reason give out personal information such as your address, phone number, school, or where you hang out.

So you've decided that you want to hang out with a cyberfriend in real time instead of on-line. Make plans to meet in a public place where you don't usually hang out by yourself. (If the meeting goes badly, you don't want your favorite snack joint to feel creepy or unsafe). Pick a mall or a movie theater or a park where there's sure to be lots of other people. Always—no matter what—bring a responsible adult with you. Tell your friend that you are bringing an adult, and insist that she does too. With a little luck, you'll have a new bud to hang with.

The Internet is an awesome place to connect with new buds and stay in touch with old ones. But like life, it's not all fun and games. The Net can, however, make your life easier. By using the Net, you can get your homework done better and, yes, faster, too. Whether you're looking for information on Chinese art or North American tree frogs, it's all there. Sounds great, right? Well, sometimes too much information is no better than none at all. The Internet is so huge that finding exactly what you're looking for can be a challenge. What to do? Read on.

Ladies, Start Your Engines

A search engine does just that—it searches. It's a program that allows you to type in keywords, then

Non-case sensitive: Most search engines are non-case sensitive. This means that you can type in terms in all capital letters, all lowercase, or a mix of both. It doesn't matter.

goes out on the Web and finds sites about these keywords. For example, if you want to find out about women in the American Civil War, you may type something like "Civil War and Women." The search engine will give you a list of sites that mention both of those topics. It lists the sites that match your request most closely first.

Search engines tend to find too much information and leave you to sort through it all yourself. They also find a lot of useless sites. These sites may contain your keywords but be about a totally different topic. The key to successful searching on the Net is to narrow your search.

For example, searching for "Civil War and Women" could find sites about the English civil war or the Spanish civil war. So you don't get all that stuff, you'll want to add "American" or "United States" to your keywords.

Search engines offer tips on how to find what you're looking for. Also, most search engines use something called boolean operators. These

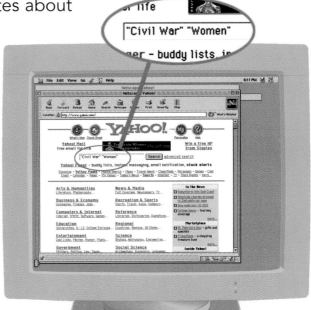

Search Engines and Internet Indexes

About.com
http://www.about.com

Let real people search for you! Real, live editors check out Web sites to decide what is worth linking to

Snap http://www.snap.com

Search engine and index for young users.

Who? Where?
http://whowhere.lycos.com/

Internet phone book of e-mail addresses.

Yahoo http://www.yahoo.com

Popular search engine indexed by category or topic.

are special keywords that limit and define your search in certain ways. "And" and "or" are two of the most common operators.

For example, searching for "apples and oranges" would return a list of sites that mention both fruits. Searching for "apples or oranges" would return a list of sites that just mention apples, or that mention only oranges. Got it? Boolean operators make searching easier and quicker. It takes some practice, but you'll get the hang of it way fast.

Look It Up!

Why search if you don't have to? There are ways to make life easier. Some sites already have done a lot of the searching and organizing for you.

These sites, sometimes known as indexes, break the Internet down into chunks. They use categories and subcategories to help you browse and find what you're looking for. Indexes can search too, but instead of searching the whole Internet, they search through the contents of their own sites.

Yahoo, at *http://www.yahoo.com*, is one of the most popular Net indexes. It's a great place to get started. If you don't find what you're looking for there, you can try a more powerful or more specialized index or search engine. Hundreds of indexes and search engines exist, and they cover millions of topics. You'll definitely find what you want.

Gopher—Not the Animal

No, a gopher isn't the fuzzy, furry, big-toothed creature you're probably thinking of. This gopher is a special protocol. A protocol is an accepted standard for behavior and communication.

This protocol is called gopher because it tells your computer to "go fer" what you want. It's also called gopher because it was created at the University of Minnesota, whose mascot is the gopher. Gopher is used frequently in research. It's a really easy way to organize and access text documents.

You can access gopher servers with most Web

browsers, so you don't need any special software. If you're looking at a gopher server, you'll see a bunch of directories that look like folders. Inside the directories you'll see either a list of documents or more subdirectories. As you click through the directories, you burrow deeper into the server, like the furry little rodent the protocol is named for.

Goin' to the Library

Once upon a time, a book report used to mean spending endless hours in the library. Not anymore! Many libraries have their card catalogs available on-line, which is an awe-

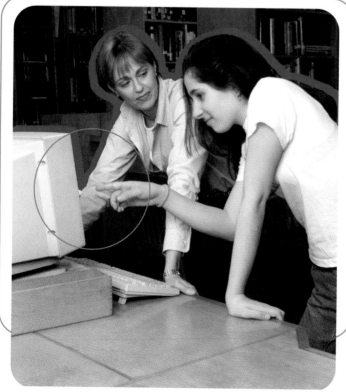

some resource when it comes time to write reports. You can search for books and find out which ones are checked out and when they're due back. Many libraries will even let you place a hold on, or reserve, checked-out books. Some will even send the books you need to the library that's closest to your house.

On-line card catalogs are easy to use. Ask your local library if they offer this service. If so, they can tell you how to connect. It's as good as going to the library, but you don't even have to put your shoes on!

Smart Stuff

Biographies of Women Mathematicians
http://www.scottlan.edu/lriddle/women/women.html
Life stories of women in math put together by math students at the Agnes Scott College in Atlanta, Georgia.

The Gutenberg Project
http://www.promo.net/pg
Project to make classic world literature available on the Net.

The Library of Congress http://www.loc.gov
The biggest library in the country, right at your fingertips. This is what the Internet is all about.

The Louvre http://mistral.culture.fr/louvre/
One of the greatest museums in the world, on-line.

The NASA Home Page http://www.nasa.gov
Download pictures and sound bites from the shuttle missions.

The Smithsonian On-line http://www.si.edu
Access all eleven of the Smithsonian museums without leaving home.

My Virtual Reference Desk
http://www.refdesk.com
Gigantic collection of information on everything you'd ever want to know.

The Young Investor
http://www.younginvestor.com/
$$$Cha-Ching$$$ It's never too soon to start learning about money.

Shop 'til You Drop

Whatever you're shopping for, from clothing to CDs to computer software, you'll find it on-line. Go to the mall without leaving your bedroom. Pick out some cool clothes and hot music and have it delivered straight to your door.

The Internet is a fun, safe, and convenient way to shop. It's also an easy way to get ripped off. Scam artists surf the Net, just as you do. To protect yourself, you can learn to be a savvy Internet shopper.

Most people use credit cards to shop on-line. Once you've added everything you want to your virtual shopping cart, you'll be asked for your credit card information. We'll talk more about credit card purchasing a little later on. Remember: Never send cash, a money order, or a cashier's check to a business you find on the Net. Always use a credit card or personal check so you can stop payment if something goes wrong.

Shareware and Freeware

What's the best kind of shopping? Shopping for free stuff, of course! One of the best things you can get on the Net is computer software. No matter what kind of computer you have, if you're looking for software, you probably can find it on-line for free or almost free.

Thousands of sites have shareware and freeware programs just waiting for you to download them. Not only can you buy neat stuff, but you can help your computer work better, faster, whatever.

Freeware is free. 'Nuff said. You're welcome to use free-ware programs and pass them on to your friends. Shareware, however, is not free. You can download and try out a share-ware program with-out paying. If you like it—and use it— you're expected to

Computer Stuff

Tucows http://www.tucows.com

One of the best places to find freeware and shareware.

Shareware.com http://www.shareware.com

A great all-purpose shareware site.

send a payment to the program's creator. Most shareware is pretty cheap, only ten or twenty dollars. Shareware programmers make a living selling these programs, so it's important to pay them. Not paying your shareware fees is stealing, and it's not cool.

The Net has some pretty neat shareware and freeware libraries. Try http://www.shareware.com to get started.

So, Is It Safe?

A lot of people think Internet shopping is risky. Often that's because they don't understand how it works. Many people worry that a hacker will do some virtual eavesdropping and write down their credit card number as it's sent over the Net.

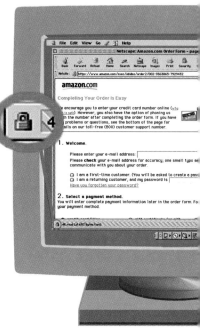

Most trustworthy on-line stores use a technology called SSL (Secure Socket Layer) to make sure this doesn't happen. An Internet server using SSL is called a secure server. Any information you send is encrypted, or scrambled, making it all but impossible to decode without the key.

Never give a credit card number over the Internet unless you're using a secure server. How do you know if a site is secure? If you're using Netscape Navigator or Microsoft Internet Explorer, look at the bottom left corner of the browser window. You'll see either a lock or a key. If the lock is closed or if the key is unbroken, you're on a secure

Where to Find It

Amazon.com

http://www.amazon.com
"The World's Biggest Bookstore" has reviews, author and publisher comments, rare-book searches, music, videos, and fun gifts.

Bloomingdale's

http://www.bloomingdales.com
The famous New York City department store, on-line!

Ebay

http://www.ebay.com
An on-line auction house where you can bid on everything from jewelry to hubcaps.

Net Grocer

http://www.netgrocer.com
Yes, you can buy potato chips and oatmeal over the Web. Your groceries are delivered straight to your door.

Shopping.com

http://www.shopping.com
Everything you'd ever want. Could you ask for more?

server. If the lock is open or if the key is broken, you're not on a secure server. If the server isn't secure, it's possible for people to listen in. Be smart—don't tell them what they want to know.

Be a Responsible Shopper

Never use your parents' credit cards without their permission. Can you say "grounded"?

If you shop on-line, you'll probably want to ask your parents to make the actual purchases for you. If you have supercool parents and they let you use their credit card, be sure you have their okay before buying anything. Tell them exactly what you are planning to purchase and

how much it costs. Then when you're done, write down the total amount you've charged on the card. Also write down the store's URL, e-mail address, phone number, and physical address so that you can contact it in case there's a problem.

Buyer Beware!

This guide lists some great places to get started shopping, and you're sure to find tons of other hot sites as you explore. On-line shopping is an awesome way to save money, so shop around and compare prices. If you aren't sure an on-line business is for real, don't give it your money. The Net has tons of great deals, but if something looks too good to be true, it probably is.

> **Encryption:** Computer encryption is so powerful that the U.S. Department of Defense classifies PGP, the encryption almost everyone uses, as a weapon.

Even More Cool Stuff

Before long, you'll be an old pro at surfing the Net. Everything you've learned so far will look like kid stuff, and you'll be ready for the big leagues. Here are just a few more things you'll want to explore as you head into cyberspace.

FTP

You'll want to have at least a clue about FTP so you don't get pegged as an Internet newbie. FTP stands for File Transfer Protocol, and it's incredibly simple. You can do two things with FTP: download files and upload files.

Downloading a file means to copy it from the Internet onto your computer. Uploading a file means to copy it from your computer onto the Internet. If you need to upload a lot of files to the

Internet, the fastest way to do it is through FTP.

Most Web browsers support the FTP protocol. In other words, you can download stuff from FTP sites without having any extra software. If you want to upload stuff, however, you'll need to get an FTP program. You can get Fetch for Macintosh or Cute FTP for PCs.

Telnet

Telnet lets you connect to a far-off computer and give commands as if you were sitting right in front of it. Why would you want to? Well, let's say you're sleeping over at a bud's house, and you want to see if your crush sent you an e-mail. She has a computer and an Internet connection, but her mail program is all set up to retrieve mail from her account. Not to worry! Just telnet.

If you're using a Web browser, type "telnet://" followed by the name of the host in the URL field. The host is usually your ISP's domain name, or the second part of your e-mail address. If you're using a telnet program, choose "connect" or "open connection" from the menu, and type in the domain name of the host. To log off, type "logout," "exit," or "bye" at the command prompt.

Beware of Viruses!

To keep your computer healthy, you'll want to avoid viruses. A virus is a computer program that sneaks into your computer through another program and can destroy it. The only way you can get a virus is from a computer program. Sometimes files, such as Microsoft Word documents, have small programs, called macros, embedded in them. To stay safe from viruses, use a virus scanning program when you download files from the Internet. These programs will examine files for viruses and warn you if a file is contaminated.

It's a myth that you can get a virus from opening an e-mail or downloading a file. You can't; you actually have to run a contaminated program on your computer.

Getting Personal

Try making your own home page! It's a great way to meet people, express yourself, and help guide others to your favorite spots on the Net. Also, most ISPs give users free space on their servers for personal home pages.

So how do you make a home page? Isn't it ultra-techno and intimidating? Not really. Web sites are created using HTML (hyper text markup language), and many programs will write this language for you. There are tons of tools out there designed to make it easy to build a home page.

If you want to make a personal page, start by looking at the sites below. They'll tell you how to plan and build your page, and they'll even help you do it. You'll find out what cool things to include—and what never, ever to put on your page. These sites also can give you info on getting your page on-line and helping people find it. Got it? Then get going! No more newbie for you, girl. You're a Netizen now!   :-)

application A computer software program designed to perform a specific task or set of tasks.

browser An application that allows you to read, or browse, files, especially Web pages.

chat A real-time conversation in cyberspace that is typed rather than spoken.

domain A particular named area of the Internet. The domain name is always part of a URL or an e-mail address.

hardware All the physical bits and pieces that make up your computer.

Internet service provider (ISP) Any company or institution that provides access to the Internet.

netiquette An informal set of rules and guidelines for acceptable behavior on the Internet.

protocol An accepted standard for behavior and communication.

search engine A Web-based program that searches the Internet for sites based on keywords entered by the user.

software Any application or program. Software sends instructions to your hardware.

uniform resource locator (URL) The place on the Internet where a particular Web page can be found. Also called Web address.

It's a Girl's World:
helpful info

Cool Web sites to check out:

Chick Click http://www.chickclick.com
A network of independent girl-powered "sites that don't fake it."

Girl Power http://www.girlpower.com
A site that encourages young women to express themselves creatively, especially through writing.

The Girl Scouts of America http://www.girlscouts.org
Info on troops in your area.

A Girl's World http://www.agirlsworld.com
A virtual clubhouse for girls.

Grrl http://www.grrl.com/main.html
Reviews, advice, and stories from grrls all over.

Seventeen On-line http://www.seventeen.com
On-line version of the popular magazine.

Building your own Web page? Here are some places to start:

BBEdit LIte http://www.barebones.com
A free HTML editor for the Macintosh.

A Beginners Guide to HTML
http://www.ncsa.uiuc.edu/General/Internet/WWW/HTMLPrimer.html
One of the best basic HTML tutorials available.

Create Your Own http://www.smplanet.com/webpage/webpage.html
Another good guide to creating your own Web site.

For more cool InfoGirl information, check out the author's Web site. She designed it just for this book!

http://www.webediting.com/infogirls

Oakes, Elizabeth H., ed. *Career Exploration on the Internet: A Student's Guide to More than 300 Web Sites!* Chicago: Ferguson, 1998.

Pedersen, Ted, et. al. *Make Your Own Web Page: A Guide for Kids.* Los Angeles, CA: Price Stern Sloan, 1998.

Polly, Jean Armour. *The Internet Kids & Family Yellow Pages: 1999 Edition.* New York: Osborne McGraw-Hill, 1998.

Sylvester, Diane. *Kids Exploring on the Net: Super Sites to Visit and Fun Things to Do.* Santa Barbara, CA: Learning Works, 1998.

Trumbauer, Lisa. *Free Stuff for Kids on the Internet.* Brookfield, CT: Millbrook Press, 1999.

Wolff, Michael, ed. *Netstudy: Your Guide to Getting Better Grades Using the Internet and Online Services.* New York: Wolff Mew Media, 1996.

Challenging Reading

Jantz, Gregory L. *Hidden Dangers of the Internet: Using It Without Abusing It.* Wheaton, IL: Harold Shaw Publishing, 1998.

Karl, Shannon, and Arthur Karl. *How to Get into Your Dream College Using the Web.* Scottsdale, AZ: Coriolis Group, 1997.

Leshin, Cynthia B. *Internet Adventures: Step-By-Step Guide to Finding and Using Educational Resources.* New York: Allyn & Bacon, 1998.

Index

About the Author

Marty Brown is a writer, editor, and professional Web developer living in Portland, Oregon. A former technophobe, she began using computers in 1985 but didn't overcome her fear of them until she entered the high-tech industry as a telephone technical support representative. After helping people troubleshoot their modem connections, programming seemed simple. She has developed many Internet sites and currently works as an intranet programmer for a local government agency. She holds a B.A. in liberal arts from The Evergreen State College in Washington state and an M.S. in publishing studies from New York University. She lives in Portland with her son, his father, and one cat.

Photo Credits

Cover photo by Thaddeus Harden; p. 7 © NCSA/University of Illinois at Urbana-Champaign; p. 9 © CERN/European Laboratory for Particle Physics; pp. 13, 19, 25, 29, 30, 34, 36, 40, 41 by Thaddeus Harden; p. 14 by Bob Rosewell; p. 20 © CORBIS; p. 33 © CORBIS/George Lepp.

Design and Layout

Laura Murawski